Editor-in-Chief and Founder:
    Lyndon H. LaRouche, Jr.
Editorial Board: *Lyndon H. LaRouche, Jr. , Helga
    Zepp-LaRouche, Robert Ingraham, Tony
    Papert, Gerald Rose, Dennis Small, Jeffrey
    Steinberg, William Wertz*
Co-Editors: *Robert Ingraham, Tony Papert*
Managing Editor: *Nancy Spannaus*
Technology: *Marsha Freeman*
Books: *Katherine Notley*
Ebooks: *Richard Burden*
Graphics: *Alan Yue*
Photos: *Stuart Lewis*
Circulation Manager: *Stanley Ezrol*

INTELLIGENCE DIRECTORS
Counterintelligence: *Jeffrey Steinberg, Michele
    Steinberg*
Economics: *John Hoefle, Marcia Merry Baker,
    Paul Gallagher*
History: *Anton Chaitkin*
Ibero-America: *Dennis Small*
Russia and Eastern Europe: *Rachel Douglas*
United States: *Debra Freeman*

INTERNATIONAL BUREAUS
Bogotá: *Miriam Redondo*
Berlin: *Rainer Apel*
Copenhagen: *Tom Gillesberg*
Houston: *Harley Schlanger*
Lima: *Sara Madueño*
Melbourne: *Robert Barwick*
Mexico City: *Gerardo Castilleja Chávez*
New Delhi: *Ramtanu Maitra*
Paris: *Christine Bierre*
Stockholm: *Ulf Sandmark*
United Nations, N.Y.C.: *Leni Rubinstein*
Washington, D.C.: *William Jones*
Wiesbaden: *Göran Haglund*

ON THE WEB
e-mail: eirns@larouchepub.com
www.larouchepub.com
www.executiveintelligencereview.com
www.larouchepub.com/eiw
Webmaster: *John Sigerson*
Assistant Webmaster: *George Hollis*
Editor, Arabic-language edition: *Hussein Askary*

EIR (ISSN 0273-6314) *is published weekly
(50 issues), by EIR News Service, Inc.,
P.O. Box 17390, Washington, D.C. 20041-0390.
(703) 777-9451*

European Headquarters: E.I.R. GmbH, Postfach
Bahnstrasse 9a, D-65205, Wiesbaden, Germany
Tel: 49-611-73650
Homepage: http://www.eirna.com
e-mail: eirna@eirna.com
Director: Georg Neudecker

Montreal, Canada: 514-461-1557

Denmark: EIR - Danmark, Sankt Knuds Vej 11,
basement left, DK-1903 Frederiksberg, Denmark.
Tel.: +45 35 43 60 40, Fax: +45 35 43 87 57. e-mail:
eirdk@hotmail.com.

Mexico City: EIR, Sor Juana Inés de la Cruz 242-2
Col. Agricultura C.P. 11360
Delegación M. Hidalgo, México D.F.
Tel. (5525) 5318-2301
eirmexico@gmail.com

Canada Post Publication Sales Agreement
#40683579

Postmaster: Send all address changes to *EIR*, P.O.
Box 17390, Washington, D.C. 20041-0390.

Signed articles in *EIR* represent the views of the
authors, and not necessarily those of the Editorial
Board.

Killer Hillary

New York Times Blows the Whistle On Killer Hillary Clinton

Feb. 29—Today the *New York Times* published a devastating documentary account of the pivotal role played by Hillary Clinton in the regime-change and assassination program carried out in 2011 against Libyan head of state Muammar Qadaffi. The detailed exposé, based on interviews with more than 50 current and former Obama Administration officials and others, makes it clear that it was Hillary Clinton, above all others, who drove the Libya overthrow, and who is more responsible than anyone else for the destruction that has followed.

If Libya has emerged as the latest beachhead for the Islamic State terrorists, blame Hillary Clinton. If Africa has become a bloody battle ground, with massive weapons spreading out from Libya all across the continent and into Syria and Iraq as well, blame Hillary Clinton. Former Defense Secretary Robert Gates quit the Obama Administration over Hillary Clinton's Libya war, and he told the *New York Times* that it was Clinton who pushed through the decision to bomb Libya, under the fraud that it was a "humanitarian" intervention, rather than the regime change that was intended all along.

Lyndon LaRouche told colleagues during the weekly LPAC Policy Committee dialogue this afternoon that the *New York Times* account presented the real picture of Hillary's role in the Libya disaster, and that role was "most ugly, evil, and astonishing." It raises some obvious questions: Who is the real Hillary Clinton? This, LaRouche warned, goes to the essence

CC/Marc Nozell

On hearing the news that Qaddafi had been murdered, two days after she had visited Libya, Hillary told press correspondents: "We came, we saw, he died."

of the matter: "What are we being sold?" The *New York Times,* LaRouche concluded, "has presented Hillary Clinton as a sold-out person. It is clear today that she was the author of the Obama killer policies." Hillary Clinton went right from being the Presidential candidate running against Barack Obama in 2008 to being the one "who did all the dirty work for Obama."

Regardless of what the *New York Times* intended, in publishing the exhaustive account of Hillary Clinton's central role in the Libya program, it has shed some critical light on what kind of disasters the world would face under a Hillary Clinton presidency.

EIR Contents

www.larouchepub.com   Volume 43, Number 10, March 4, 2016

White House/Lawrence Jackson

Cover This Week

President Barack Obama, with Secretary of State Hillary Rodham Clinton, delivers a statement in the Rose Garden of the White House, Sept. 12, 2012, regarding the attack the day before on the U.S. consulate in Benghazi, Libya.

I. The Silk Road and the Ceasefire

The Silk Road Can Make The Syrian Ceasefire Succeed

Feb. 24—When Israel and the Palestine Liberation Organization signed an agreement in 1993 to end the killing and establish self-government for the Palestinians, Lyndon LaRouche immediately said that the tractors must roll, immediately, if the plan was to succeed. The common benefit to both sides, based on Israeli industrial capacity and Palestinian skilled labor, must be launched without delay, he insisted. That did not happen, as the IMF and World Bank were put in charge to oversee the process.

Twenty-three Years Later

The dramatic ceasefire in Syria agreed to by Foreign Minister Sergei Lavrov and Secretary of State John Kerry on Feb. 22 in Munich, and confirmed in a phone call from President Vladimir Putin to President Barack Obama, has the immediate potential of transforming not only Syria, not only the Mideast, but the entire world. The brilliant strategic intervention by Putin into Syria last year demonstrated that terrorists could be defeated, but also that the United States under President Obama had in fact sided with the terrorists to achieve "regime change" against uncooperative governments. That era of U.S. subservience to British imperial tyranny can be finished—if the ceasefire holds.

As with Oslo, the ceasefire will only hold if the reconstruction and development of Syria (and the region) begins immediately. Helga Zepp-LaRouche said on Feb. 23 that the Silk Road process launched by Xi Jinping can and must be brought into the region now—not next month or next year. The development program for Southwest Asia presented in the *EIR* report, *The New Silk Road Becomes the World Land-Bridge,* provides the foundation. Xi Jinping initiated the project during his visit to Saudi Arabia, Iran, and Egypt in January. There is no time to lose.

The scope of the Syria agreement is breathtaking when contrasted with the all-out effort over the past months by London, Wall Street, and the White House to demonize Putin, threatening war on Russia both in Europe and the Mideast. After the phone call between Putin and Obama, Obama issued only a brief acknowledgement of the call. Putin, on the other hand, issued a statement elucidating the details of the historic breakthrough, worked out through "intensive work by Russian and American experts."

The agreement establishes close cooperation between U.S. and Russian "political and military officials," all under UN oversight, who will jointly establish a hot line, and a joint working group to "promote and monitor" the ceasefire. The full-scale war on al-Nusra and ISIS will continue unabated—with significant levels of U.S.-Russian cooperation.

John Kerry's spokesman, Mark Toner, asked on Feb. 22 what will happen to U.S.-backed opposition groups who continue fighting alongside ISIS and al-Nusra, responded: "If you hang out with the wrong folks, then you make that decision."

The CIA, and the White House, are not pleased. The *Wall Street Journal* issued a report from unnamed sources, that CIA Director John Brennan, Secretary of Defense Ash Carter, and Obama's new Chairman of the Joint Chiefs, Gen. Joseph Dunford, are doing what they can to sabotage the deal, claiming that Putin will not comply, and demanding new and increased pressure on him, to cause "real pain." The *Economist* magazine, the voice of the City of London, went berserk, writing: "The only puzzle is what John Kerry, America's secretary of state, thought he could achieve through his agreement with Mr Lavrov—except, perhaps, to expose Russian cynicism."

Clearly, leading figures within the U.S. institutions realized that if Obama were allowed to proceed, the world would be rapidly heading for thermonuclear extinction. Now, there are those who want to dump him, as well we must. What is required to consolidate these moves, is to end the power of the problem at the source—Wall Street and the British empire. Unleashing the global development process required, must begin by shutting down Wall Street and restoring a sane economic order.

A Peace Plan for Southwest Asia

by Helga Zepp-LaRouche

WASHINGTON, Feb. 26, 2016—It may be a happy coincidence or divine providence, that the Arabic translation of our World Land-Bridge book comes out just as the prospect of a ceasefire in Syria is becoming a reality. The accord between U.S. Secretary of State John Kerry and Russian Foreign Minister Sergey Lavrov has the potential of bringing a war of five years, which cost hundreds of thousands of human lives, to an end. But given the enormous intricacies of the region, it should also be clear that a mere contract to stop fighting will be too fragile to last and survive new provocations, by the same forces which were responsible for the war.

EIRNS/Christopher Lewis

Helga Zepp-LaRouche speaking at an EIR *conference in Frankfurt, Germany, April 2015.*

The only way that a durable peace can be guaranteed, is to immediately launch a comprehensive development plan for all of Southwest Asia, with an integrated infrastructure development plan, which not only reconstructs the cities and villages destroyed by the war, but which takes a much more fundamental approach to return this region, which was one of the cradles of human civilization and at various points in history harbored the most developed cultures of the time, to one of the most advanced regions of the world again. The aim must be to unleash the creativity of the people of the region and bring their productivity up to the level of Europe, the United States, or China.

This is absolutely possible, most emphatically because Russia, China, and India are the powerful neighbors which, in collaboration and together with the countries of the region, can bring this development about. If the development projects proposed in this report are implemented, starting literally tomorrow, so that the peace dividend becomes visible for all sides in the region, then the ceasefire in Syria and the implementation of what one could call a Silk Road-Marshall Plan, without a cold war connotation however, can become a game-changer for the whole world.

At a moment when the refugee crisis is threatening to become an unprecedented humanitarian crisis, detonating the cohesion and possibly even the existence of the European Union, a vision of hope to develop Southwest Asia and Africa is the only way to turn the situation around. At a moent when the financial system of the trans-Atlantic world is about to crash, the development perspective to rebuild the Near and Middle East to become the bridge between Asia, Europe, and Africa, is the only engine of economic growth to prevent Europe and the United States from going down in chaos.

So on the realization of this program, the fate of all of humanity depends.

The Silk Road as the New Paradigm for All Mankind

by Helga Zepp-LaRouche

Mrs. Zepp-LaRouche addressed the 2016 Global Chinatown Conference Seattle Summit & Global Fortune Innovation Development Promotion Fair in Seattle on Feb. 24, sponsored by the North America China Council. She had pre-recorded these remarks on Feb. 21.

Dear Ladies and Gentlemen, dear participants in this very important conference:

I'm very happy to speak to you about the Silk Road as the New Paradigm for All of Mankind. It is the beautiful characteristic of the human being that we are, unlike the animals, not forced to walk in trodden ways, and repeat from generation to generation what was done before. But what distinguishes us from all other species on this planet, is that we can look at the situation from above, in its totality; we can analyze it, and if there is something wrong with the way things are going, we have the freedom to change it and create a new paradigm.

And the world is in a very urgent need of having a new paradigm, because if you look at the old one, what do we see? We have a new Cold War which could be transformed into a hot war at a moment's notice. You could have a full-fledged confrontation between NATO and Russia and China, quickly developing into a new world war. The situation is characterized by many experts as more dangerous today than at the height of the Cold War, and that was the Cuban Missile Crisis.

NATO has a military buildup at the Russian border of a dimension not seen since 1941, when the Nazis invaded the Soviet Union. Russia is responding to that by moving its heavy military equipment to its western border, including tactical nuclear weapons. And if the Turkish crisis escalates, and Turkey moves ground troops into Syria, where there is now a little ray of hope because of the recent agreement between Secretary of State Kerry and Foreign Minister Lavrov,— but if this were to happen, and Turkey invaded Syria against the Kurdish north, you could quickly have a war between a NATO member, Turkey, and Russia.

But also, if you look at the tensions in the South China Sea and the increasing escalation around the Korean Peninsula, these situations are extremely dan-

army.mil

"NATO has a military buildup at the Russian border of a dimension not seen since 1941." Here, NATO troops in a military exercise on June 9, 2015 in the Drawsko Pomorskie Training Area in Northwest Poland.

U.S. Navy Photo/Mass Communication Specialist 3rd Class Declan Barnes

The Obama Administration has been escalating tension in the South China Sea. Here, guided missile destroyer USS Curtis Wilbur is underway in the Philippine Sea in 2013, as part of the Washington Carrier Strike Group, in operations in the Indo-Asia-Pacific region.

gerous and worrisome. If it comes at any moment to an escalation of any one of these regional conflicts, and nuclear weapons were used,— which is absolutely not impossible,— it would be the logic of such a war that it would lead to a complete and total thermonuclear exchange, which obviously would lead to the annihilation of the human species.

Financial Blowout, Refugee Crisis

There is a second aspect of this crisis: We are on the edge of a new blowout of the financial system, which would make the 2008 crisis pale by comparison. William White, who is the former chief economist of the Bank for International Settlements (BIS), just recently stated what is obvious: that the total outstanding debt of the world is unpayable, and that we must have, as in the Jubilee in many religions over the last 5,000 years, a complete writedown of all these unpayable debts. The alternative would be the immediate implementation of Franklin D. Roosevelt's Glass-Steagall banking separation law. If that is not done,— and White puts it in these words,— he says: "Either it's done in an orderly fashion, or it will come to a chaotic collapse."

The meltdown of the financial system in slices is already going on since the beginning of the year. Market mechanisms don't function any more, and the famous tools which were used in the 2008 crisis—quantitative easing, bail-out/bail-in, even negative interest rates— they have turned out to be not only not ineffective, but counterproductive by worsening the deflationary spiral which is now underway in the entire trans-Atlantic sector and in Japan.

The third aspect of the strategic crisis is the unprecedented refugee crisis, which emanates from mainly the Middle East, but also Africa. According to the United Nations, there are 60 million people already moving, fleeing from war and hunger, including over 5 million people from Syria alone. The director of the Davos World Economic Forum, Claus Schwab, said if we don't change course, there will be *1 billion people* coming soon from war-torn regions.

Now, I don't want to list more aspects of this crisis, which I easily could do. But if you only consider those I mentioned, it should be clear that we have an unprecedented civilizational crisis confronting us.

The good news is that the New Paradigm already exists. In September 2013, President Xi Jinping of China declared the New Silk Road to be the official policy of China, in the tradition of the ancient Silk Road, exchanging not only goods and culture, but also technologies,— and this, he said, should be based on a "win-win" cooperation by simply expanding the Chinese economic miracle to all countries who want to cooperate.

Anyone who ever was in China will confirm that the Chinese economic miracle of the last 30 years in particular, is absolutely breathtaking. China has completed a development in 30 years, for which the industrial countries of the trans-Atlantic regions required 150 or even 200 years. China has lifted 800 million out of poverty, and the goal is to develop the western part of China to eliminate poverty by the year 2020 altogether.

The New Silk Road project is already becoming the largest development scheme ever, on this Earth. Already $600 billion in investments are envisioned, with the Chinese intending to invest $1 trillion equivalent in the next years in other countries. In the two and a half years since Xi Jinping announced the New Silk Road, it is developing with breathtaking speed: Sixty countries are already cooperating in it. Since January 16, the Asian Infrastructure Investment Bank (AIIB) has started to function in Beijing, providing credits to countries that require them. So they have launched construction projects, including the transcontinental railway from Yiwu and Chongqing to Europe with the cooperation of the countries along the way; they're building the Greek port of Piraeus, and the Jakarta-Bandung high-speed railway. The first cargo train just arrived on Feb. 15, from Yiwu to Tehran, with 32 containers, which was the result of Xi Jinping's visit to Iran earlier.

In 2015, China invested in 49 countries along the "One Belt, One Road" New Silk Road. It invested, according to the Commerce Ministry, $14.8 billion, in 3,987 projects! It has in contracts with 60 countries. All these projects will have tremendous economic benefits during this year, during 2016, and therefore, the narrative that it is the Chinese "slowdown" which is responsible for the tumult in the trans-Atlantic sector is completely nonsensical.

President Xi Jinping offered at the APEC meeting in October 2014, to President Obama, cooperation between China and the United States on the basis of such a "win-win" perspective. And that *is* the solution.

Why are we, then, on the verge of World War III?

Xinhua/Wang Ye

Chinese President Xi Jinping delivering a speech at the Nazarbayev University in Astana, Kazakstan, Sept. 7, 2013, announcing the Silk Road policy. The New Silk Road Project is becoming the largest development scheme ever, with an envisioned $600 billion in investments. Sixty countries are already cooperating in it.

Our Proposal of 1991

We have to go back to '91, at the time of the collapse of the Soviet Union, because at that time, there was the real chance to develop the peace order for the Twenty-first Century. But, it was missed. There was the possibility, because the enemy,— Communism, the Soviet Union,— had disappeared—but it was not taken. The Schiller Institute, however, at that point, made a proposal which we called the Eurasian Land-Bridge, the New Silk Road, which was the idea of connecting the population and industrial centers of Europe with those of Asia through "development corridors," and in this way, uplift the productivity of all the landlocked areas of the Eurasian continent.

We proposed this. It would have been the basis for a peace order, and we have campaigned for this in the 25 years since, in hundreds of conferences and seminars. And therefore, we were very happy when it finally was put on the agenda by Xi Jinping.

Now, despite promises at that time not to extend NATO to the borders of Russia, which was testified to many times by the former American ambassador to Moscow, Jack Matlock,— unfortunately what dominated at that point was the Wolfowitz-Cheney doctrine, which was the idea that, okay, now the United States is the only superpower left, and it must be guaranteed that never will a country or a group of countries be able to challenge that status of the United States, as the only superpower.

The development of the last 25 years also demonstrates very clearly that this is not the reality, that you have emerging countries, especially China, and also India, who are rising; you have Russia regaining its military strength. And therefore, the idea that a unipolar world is possible, is simply not realistic.

However, a *multipolar* world is also not the solution, because the idea of a multipolar world still remains in the geometry of geopolitics, and it was that geopolitics which was the cause for two world wars of the 20th Century.

We are therefore in need of a new paradigm which overcomes geopolitics from a higher order. Nikolaus of Cusa, the eminent thinker of the 15th Century, basically defined that solutions which are real solutions can never be partial, heterogenic solutions, but must address the commonality of the problem by the method of the *coincidentia oppositorum*, the coincidence of opposites. It's the principle that the One has a higher order of magnitude than the Many, and that it is possible on a higher level of reason to conceptualize a solution in which the contradictions of the lower level never exist.

One can create a new paradigm which is exactly of the dimension of the paradigm-shift from the Middle Ages, which was dominated by scholasticism, by the Peripatetics, by the Aristotelian idea that a thing can not be A and not-A, or that there is *always* a contradiction between A and B.

So this change, which Nikolaus of Cusa introduced by this new method of thinking, led to modern natural science, Classical art, the new role of the individual, and everything that has proven human creativity to be the driving force in the physical universe through a limitless possibility of *inventions* and discovery of new physical principles.

It is exactly such a fundamental paradigm shift, like that which divides the Middle Ages from modern times, which is required today. We have to make the evolutionary jump, from geopolitics to the common aims of mankind. And obviously this requires a vision of where should mankind be in 100 years, 1,000 years, or even 10,000 years from now? If one considers the enormous progress mankind has made in the last 10,000 years, from Stone Age conditions to today being able to communicate with little "smart phones" in conferences in which you can see your partners all over the world,— just to mention one little example,— should we not be able to solve the problems of mankind on a completely different level?

Should we not be able to pull back from the brink of thermonuclear war and join hands and solve the problem of war, hunger, and terrorism? When President Xi was recently in Southwest Asia, in Saudi Arabia, Egypt, and Iran, he offered the expansion of the New Silk Road, the One Belt, One Road policy, as a Noah's Ark for the refugee crisis.

The Common Aims of Mankind

The Schiller Institute already in 2012 had convened a conference in Frankfurt, Germany, where we presented a comprehensive plan to develop the entire Middle East from Afghanistan to the Mediterranean, from the Caucasus to the Persian Gulf, and to have real economic development for this region as a perspective to overcome poverty, war, and the grounds for the recruitment to terrorism! It was the idea of declaring a "war on the desert" by developing new, huge amounts of clean water through the desalination of ocean water with the help of nuclear energy, and by tapping into the moisture of the atmosphere through ionization; of developing new agriculture and forestry, of developing infrastructure, linking the new cities which have to be built, so that the entire region becomes one of the prosperous, beautiful regions of the world.

Such a perspective, naturally, is easy. It would be very easy if Russia, China, India, Iran, and Egypt, *and* European nations, such as Italy, Germany, and France, joined hands, and hopefully would even get the United States to cooperate, to together develop this region. And this is the *only* way that we can end the refugee crisis, by developing that part of the world, and naturally, also Africa.

And it would be very, very easy, with what you could call a "Silk Road Marshall Plan" and a "win-win" perspective.

Some of the common aims of mankind are also within reach in the not so distant future. For example, we can reach energy and raw-materials security: This would be possible through the realization of thermonuclear fusion power, which is now very, very close. Recently, there were two breakthroughs: One in Germany in Greifswald, where the Wendelstein 7-X Stellarator test reactor was able, for one-tenth of a second, to heat plasma to several million degrees. And the goal in Greifswald is to have a 30-minute stable plasma by 2020.

The same day, reports were coming from the Institute for Plasma Physics in Hebei, a province near Beijing, that the experiment with the the Experimental Advanced Superconducting Tokamak (EAST) reactor, was able to maintain a plasma for 102 seconds at 50

Fusion power will give the world power and energy security and raw materials security. The second generation of fusion power is already part of the Chinese lunar mission Chang'e-5. Artist's conception of the Chang'e-5 lunar sample return vehicle is shown here.

CCTV

million degrees, which is half what is necessary for fusion of deuterium and tritium, and they have the goal of reaching a plasma of 100 million degrees temperature, in a stable condition. The results of this EAST experiment will be applied at ITER in France, at the joint international project.

Fusion power will give the world power and energy security *and* raw materials security, because with the accompanying fusion torch procedure, you can basically transform all waste into new isotopes, and create new raw materials!

The second generation of fusion power is already part of the Chinese lunar mission Chang'e-5, which will go into orbit in 2017. It's designed to bring back the first samples of fusion-ready helium-3 as a preparation for the future industrial exploitation of the Moon. Helium-3 as a fuel will also mean a new revolution in energy generation, because it will be possible to convert its energy directly into electricity at much higher efficiency levels; it will also revolutionize space travel as a fuel.

One of the most exciting common aims of mankind is space research in general. The Chinese converted the Chang'e-4 lunar mission, which was designed to be the backup for the very successful Chang'e-3, into a landing mission on the so-called "dark side of the Moon," for 2018: This will be the first time mankind has placed an object on the far side of the Moon. It will enable China to have a large radio telescope where the Moon, on the far side, is shielded from radio interference from Earth,— and that part of the Moon also has the highest concentration of helium-3.

But even more important, it will give mankind for the first time, a much deeper insight into the Solar system and beyond, and into our Galaxy, and the many galaxies out there.

So therefore, let the United States join the Silk Road. The United States is in urgent need of modernizing its infrastructure. The United States probably needs 50,000 miles of high-speed rail, of which China has already built 20,000 and wants to have 50,000 by the year 2020. The United States could also very well have new, beautiful cities, new fresh water to fight the drought in the Southwest; the United States should revive NASA, and it would be very easy to convert that part of production which is now used for military purposes, to convert it into other high-technology areas.

And if the United States joined the Silk Road, the United States—we—could develop all of South America, Central America, and in that way, halt the refugee crisis at the southern border of the United States; there are presently 11 million illegal immigrants in the United States, and probably the same number in desperate condition south of the border.

Mankind is at an extremely important crossroads in its existence, and we have to elevate our thinking to a much higher level if our species is to continue to exist. Let us therefore revive the American dream; let us build the New Silk Road into a World Land-Bridge, which we have proposed as a study, which really gives a blueprint for every part of the world to develop.

Let's revive the American dream and join with the Chinese dream to become the dream of all mankind.

Beijing to Seattle Through The Bering Strait

by David Christie

China's New Silk Road policy was prominently featured during the 2016 Global Chinatown Conference Seattle Summit & Global Fortune Innovation Development Promotion Fair in Seattle, Washington, on Feb. 24, sponsored by the North America China Council. The "One Belt One Road," as it is commonly referred to, was referenced by academics, investment strategists, and representatives of the Chinese Government during the course of the Seattle summit, and Helga Zepp-LaRouche addressed the conference via a 24-minute video, capturing the essence the importance of the Silk Road as a new paradigm for humanity.

The discussion of the New Silk Road in Seattle also intersected a breakout week for the policy in the "Other Washington," Washington, D.C. Lyndon LaRouche's close associates took part in a panel presentation at Georgetown University Feb. 25-26, where Matthew Ogden and Mike Billington presented the new paradigm

EIRNS/Julien Lemaître

Helga Zepp-LaRouche addressed the conference, portraying the importance of the Silk Road as a new paradigm to prevent the catastrophe now confronting mankind. Here Zepp-LaRouche is shown at a 2007 World Land-Bridge conference with Engineer Hal Cooper, a proponent of the project. Cooper also attended the Seattle summit.

for peace through economic development at a conference entitled "Revolution of the Global Economy," organized by public policy graduate students. LaRouche associate Matthew Ogden was invited to present the new paradigm of the Silk Road policy on the keynote panel of the conference, along with Brookings Fellow Alice Rivlin, the former Vice Chair of the Federal Reserve and former head of the Office of Management and Budget, as well as former Senator Byron Dorgan, a 30-year member of Congress from North Dakota. Rivlin referred to Ogden as "the ultimate optimist," after Ogden had said that China's One Belt One Road policy was fulfilling the dream of Franklin D. Roosevelt.

The Seattle discussion that featured "The Silk Road Lady," Helga Zepp-LaRouche, in parallel with that of Lyndon LaRouche's close associates at Georgetown University, also occurred while Chinese Foreign Minister Wang Yi made a profound intervention in Washington, D.C. Wang Yi intersected the breakthrough agreement on the cessation of hostilities in Syria, organized chiefly by Secretary of State John Kerry and Russian Foreign Minister Sergey Lavrov, which passed unanimously in the United Nations Security Council.

Foreign Minister Wang Yi then went on to give a presentation Feb. 25 at the Center for Strategic and International Studies (CSIS), where he cited the Belt and Road policy as the only path for peace in the Middle East as Xi Jinping's trip there earlier this year highlighted—what some now refer to as a "new Marshall Plan." Wang Yi also called on China and the United States to cooperate on the New Silk Road policy, which was an echo of Chinese President Xi Jinping's offer to U.S. President Barack Obama at the APEC Summit in 2014 to join the Asian Infrastructure and Investment Bank (AIIB) and the Silk Road Fund.

Matthew Ogden (shown above) of LaRouche PAC took part in a Feb. 25-26 Georgetown University conference entitled "Revolution of the Global Economy." He presented the new paradigm of the Silk Road policy on the keynote panel. On the right, speakers Alice Rivlin, a former U.S. Federal Reserve and budget official, and former U.S. Senator Byron Dorgan (D-ND).

LPAC/Alicia Cerretani

Instead of accepting Xi's offer in 2014 for peace and economic development, Obama has moved the world to the edge of thermonuclear annihilation with his Asia Pivot and NATO's encirclement of Russia. While saner forces within the institution of the Presidency have now moved to contain Obama, as John Kerry's recent breakthrough in Syria indicates, Lyndon LaRouche has warned that unless Obama is removed from office, that danger of extinction remains. LaRouche has also called for the end of the British empire and its branch office in Wall Street, so that the United States can join Russia, China, and India in the new paradigm. The United States' entry into the new paradigm of the Silk Road lies symbolically, and literally, across the Bering Strait, to unite Eurasia with North America. The Bering Strait project was prominently featured at the Global Chinatown Summit in Seattle.

Seattle Summit

The 2016 Global Chinatown Conference Seattle Summit & Global Fortune Innovation Development Promotion Fair, sponsored by the North America China Council, is part of an effort by the leadership within the Chinese American community and U.S. business and community leaders more generally, to make the policies of the Chinese government better known among Americans. Similar conferences have taken place in China, and further conferences are being planned on the West Coast of the United States, and perhaps beyond.

At the gala banquet at China Harbor Restaurant in Seattle that celebrated the start of the conference, Vice President of the China Investment Association, Hui-

yong Liu, who was part of the Beijing delegation to the Seattle summit, stated the importance of cooperation between China and the United States, and also stated that China would like to invest in the United States, particularly in U.S. infrastructure. Joint ventures between Chinese and American companies are already taking place, notably in the high-speed railway that will connect Los Angeles to Las Vegas. Many participants at the Seattle Global Chinatown Conference were excited to learn of the vision illustrated in the new LaRouche PAC pamphlet, "The United States Joins the New Silk Road," which outlines 42,000 miles of modernized electrified rail, 17,000 miles of which will be high-speed rail. Perhaps the most exciting concept to the participants of the Seattle Summit, was the Bering Strait tunnel connection, which many of the participants realized as a direct route, since the flight path from Seattle to Beijing goes right over the Bering Strait.

The conference covered many diverse topics, including investment, finance, and economy, the Trans-Pacific Partnership, and smart cities. The New Silk Road was a current that ran through various presentations at the conference, but was especially highlighted in the morning general session on Wednesday, Feb. 24. Dave Christie of the LaRouche PAC Policy Committee moderated that session, which included representatives of business, industry, and science, including from the Pacific Northwest National Laboratory, as well as Junsheng Wang of the Beijing delegation, and representatives of the Schiller Institute and *EIR*. Helga Zepp-LaRouche delivered an extremely hard-hitting video address, which reviewed the imminent danger of the strategic crisis, from the collapse of the trans-Atlantic financial system, to the refugee crisis, to the danger of thermonuclear annihilation (see the full transcript of her speech in this issue of *EIR*), but then clearly laid out the importance of the new paradigm which China is playing a leading role in developing—not just with the New Silk Road, but also the Chinese lunar program and

On Feb. 25, China Foreign Minister Wang Yi called for the Belt and Road policy as the only path to peace in the Middle East, in an address at Center for Strategic and International Studies in Washington, D.C. He met several American officials during his visit.

Xinhua/Bao Dandan

the related fusion research. She stated that the only way to create peace was with the new paradigm, and reviewed her role in the project over a 25-year period, that is now coming to fruition. In addition to reviewing the breakthroughs in fusion research and space exploration, she also discussed the issue of creativity *per se,* reviewing the method of Nicolaus of Cusa and his *Coincidentia Oppositorum* (coincidence of opposites), which demolished the system of Aristotle that had placed mental shackles on Europe, and created the basis for the Renaissance. Some of the Chinese participants were eagerly taking pictures of Zepp-LaRouche and the various maps that depicted the route of the Belt and Road.

EIR's Washington, D.C. Bureau Chief, Bill Jones, elaborated the concept of peace through economic development, and cited the lesson of the Treaty of Westphalia as the crucial forebear of Chinese President Xi Jinping's "win-win" concept, which is a basis for bringing the diverse nations together in harmony along the Silk Road. Dr. Hal Cooper presented the Bering Strait tunnel project and the related high-speed rail grid for the United States as it joins the New Silk Road.

The morning summit session also included a presentation by the Deputy Director of the Central Economic Committee of the China Democratic League, Junsheng Wang, who is also affiliated with the China Investment Association. Both Jusheng Wang and Huiyong Liu mentioned the New Silk Road on numerous occasions in the course of their various presentations in breakout sessions, and Liu mentioned the policy in his keynote that started the conference. Wang focused much of his speech on the importance of energy in the Belt and Road initiative. Wang also raised the importance of the defense of the Yuan against currency speculation in a breakout session the previous day. Farzam Kamalabadi, president and chairman of the board of Future Trends, also underlined the importance of the New Silk Road throughout the course of the conference, and highlighted the Belt and Road initiative in his keynote address to the conference body. Kamalabadi has not only promoted the Silk Road concept for many years, but also Chinese culture more generally, including poetry and calligraphy.

Seattle and China: 1979 to the Present

In his speech at the gala banquet to open the conference, Huiyong Liu of the China Investment Association told of his "rectangular" trip around the corners of the United States over the month of February, looking for potential areas of investment in Southern California, Florida, the east coast, and Seattle. Liu continued to express the same enthusiasm in Seattle that the leadership of China has shown since Deng Xiaoping's trip to Seattle in 1979, which was followed by Jiang Zemin in 1993, Hu Jintao in 2006, and by last year's visit by Xi Jinping.

Seattle, of course, is home to an impressive array of global corporations that either started in Seattle, or continue to operate in Seattle, such as Starbucks, Amazon, Costco, UPS, Paccar, Microsoft, Weyerhaeuser, and of course Boeing; every Chinese leader from Deng Xiaoping to Xi Jinping has toured Boeing's Everett facility. Washington also has an impressive array of agricultural products, which is another reason why Washington continues to rank at the top of the list of states that do business with China. In 2014, Washington State sold $20 billion worth of airplanes, apples, wheat, and other products to China.

Washington State also has an important history of nuclear science and industry with the Hanford Nuclear Reservation, which was started as part of the Manhattan Project. Research and development, power generation, and fuel enrichment still continue at Hanford, although vastly reduced after years of assault under the British imperial policy of environmentalism. In addition to commercial aircraft, Seattle also has played an important role historically in NASA, and the lunar rover of the Apollo program was tested in Kent Valley, which is today home to many private space operations oriented around space tourism. Even though these firms would cease to exist without an immortal mission for mankind as a space faring species, they could never survive solely for pleasure tours for billionaires. There is a place for their scientists and engineers in a revitalized NASA, rebuilt from its destruction under Obama.

Seattle to Beijing via The Bering Strait

In spherical geometry, the shortest distance from point A to point B on the surface of a sphere is always the great circle. According to spherical geometry, the shortest path from Seattle to Beijing brings you across the Bering Strait, more or less. The proposal to connect Russia and Alaska across this body of water goes back to the 1800s, and *EIR* has detailed the history of this idea over the past several decades.

If the Bering Strait tunnel and related railway corridors were put on a fast-track mobilization, it could be completed in about five years, although conservative estimates put completion off to more like ten or fifteen years. A study put out in 2007 by an advisor to the Russian Ministry of Economic Development and Trade, Viktor Razbegin, estimated the cost of the project to be about $60 billion. Dr. Hal Cooper, who addressed the Global Chinatown Summit in Seattle on the subject of the Bering Strait tunnel, estimates that freight delivery time would be cut from the approximately 30 days via ship, to 8 days via rail!

The Bering Strait connection would also open up an

EIRNS

Dave Christie (shown here), a member of the LaRouche PAC Policy Committee, moderated the Silk Road session of the conference.

era of development in the Arctic, an area rich in mineral and energy resources, but impossible to develop without transportation and development corridors, like the New Silk Road. The development of the Arctic region, including the development of NAWAPA XXI for inter-basin water management, would effectively become a subsidiary of the space program—conditions are so brutal, that they are akin to situations faced in space exploration, and thus provide a convenient laboratory for research.

Perhaps more important, the Bering Strait tunnel would be one of the greatest symbols of the coming end of British imperial geopolitical operations, when the United States joins Russia, China, and India for a new era of peace through development, with participation of our friends in Canada. Once these development corridors come down from the Arctic regions, they can be extended down the west coast into California, Mexico, Central America, and across the Darien Gap into South America, linking the planet from the tip of South America to the tip of South Africa.

Last year, the head of Russian Railways at that time, Vladimir Yakunin, re-proposed the Bering Strait connection, as Russia has done many times in the past. Wang Mengshu, a prominent rail expert in China, also made clear China's interest in the project last year. This project of peace was rejected by Barack Obama, in service to her Majesty, and instead, the world sits at the edge of global war. Let us now break ground, or tundra, on this great project, and drive a railroad stake through the British imperial geopolitical games forever.

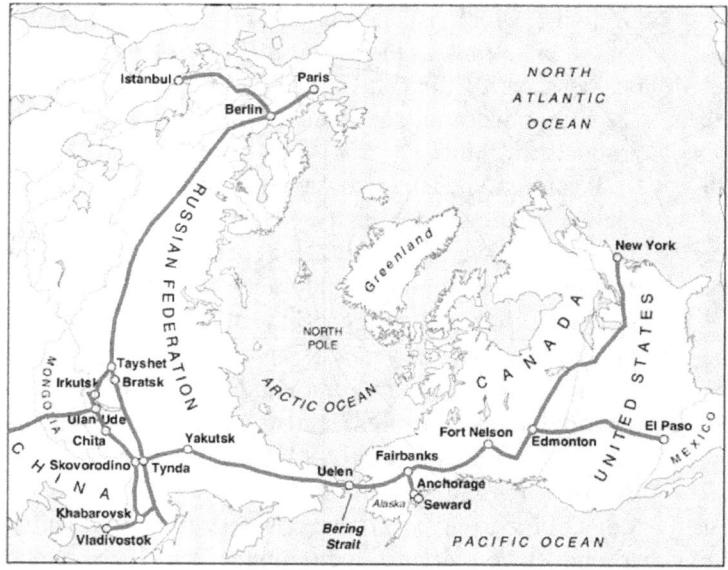

larouche.se

The shortest distance from Seattle to Beijing is along the great circle which crosses near the Bering Strait.

The Secret to China's Rise— A Question of Leadership

by Jeffrey Steinberg and William Jones

Feb. 29—In a United States now become a post-industrial rust-bucket, the entire list of current "major" presidential candidates is characterized more by the candidates' over-riding ambition rather than their political— and moral—qualifications to lead a country. At the same time, the world has been amazed by the tremendous growth of the Chinese economy and by the unprecedented capability to bring 600 million people out of poverty between 1981 and 2004. What is the secret to this "Chinese miracle," and does it hold lessons for us, and perhaps an admonishment, as we go to elections with a lackluster group of mere politicians?

The key to the mystery is the quality of leadership shown in recent times by the people who have been called upon to steer the ship of state in the People's Republic of China. We must begin by looking at the man who was single-handedly responsible for the "reform and opening up" which shifted China onto the track of rapid economic development, Deng Xiaoping.

Deng Xiaoping with Mao Zedong in 1975. Mao died in 1976 and the Cultural Revolution died with him. Deng came to power in 1977.

Deng Xiaoping Takes the Reins

By the time Deng Xiaoping took control of the Communist Party of China (CPC), following the death of Mao Zedong and the arrests of the Gang of Four, China had gone through a period of 40 years of devastation. For China, the Second World War began in 1937, with the Japanese invasion. Over the next dozen years, China was in a state of continuous warfare—warfare against the Japanese through 1945, and then the civil war, which lasted until Chaing Kai-shek's forces were driven from the mainland in 1949.

At the end of World War II, the average life expectancy in China was 41 years. Over the course of the next three decades, between the Great Leap Forward and the Cultural Revolution, China destroyed itself.

The educational system, including the entire university system, was virtually shut down. China's most educated scientists, teachers, engineers, and medical professionals were shipped to the countryside for "re-education," a euphemism for slave labor and mental torture, or had been killed in the hysterical purges by the Red Guards.

Deng Xiaoping, a hero of the Chinese Revolution, was purged from power three times. He suffered personal tragedy during the Cultural Revolution, when his son was denied medical care and wound up paralyzed for life.

He persevered, and when he was returned to "active party work" following Mao's death, he knew exactly what he had to do to rebuild China to its former greatness—and beyond. For Deng Xiaoping, the key to China's future was to launch a scientific revolution. He told close friends and party colleagues that he intended to devote almost all of his time to reviving China's scien-

Zhou Enlai "had always served as a beacon of hope during the dark days of the Cultural Revolution." Here, Zhou (center) with Saifuddin Azizi, the first chairman of the Xinjiang Uyghur Autonomous Region (right), in 1965. Zhou died a few months before Mao in 1976.

Mao's Death and Deng's Revolution

With the death of Mao Zedong on September 6, 1976 and the arrests the following month of the "Gang of Four," Deng Xiaoping rapidly established himself as China's new "supreme leader." Despite the fact that the only formal top position he would hold was as Chairman of the Central Military Commission, it was Deng's vision of a modern China that was the single most significant factor in the revolutionary changes that China underwent in the next 40 years.

According to Deng biographer Ezra Vogel, from the moment he returned to power, Deng Xiaoping prioritized the development of a scientific and technological cadre over all other responsibilities and initiatives. He emphasized to colleagues that if China were able to train a generation of world-class scientists and engineers, then within 30 years, China would be able to emerge as a leading nation.

In pursuit of this enormous goal, Deng completed the normalization of relations with the United States that had begun with the 1972 Kissinger-Nixon diplomatic opening. On January 1, 1979, the United States officially recognized the People's Republic of China as the one China.

Deng knew the magnitude of the challenge that China was facing in this regard. Following the start of the Cultural Revolution, nearly an entire generation of young people were deprived of any higher education.

The campaign of the Gang of Four against "bourgeois intellectuals" led to restrictions on students not from a worker or peasant background and the loss of a good portion of the teaching cadres, many of whom of "bourgeois background" were sent to the country to perform manual work and be "re-educated." Chairman Mao called for shorter study times, and demanded that the students who finished their course work return to work in the factories or on the collective farms. Although there were still some universities in operation during that period, the level was far below what it had been or would later become.

This was the situation for almost ten years. Then in 1977, when the first of the Deng Xiaoping reforms were

tific and educational systems. If he succeeded, he observed confidently, China would re-emerge as a great nation within 30 years.

The stage had been set by Zhou Enlai. While Zhou had always served as a beacon of hope during the dark days of the Cultural Revolution, he died a few months before the death of Mao in 1976. In 1975, Zhou had formulated the policy of the "four modernizations" as a program for bringing China out of the devastation wreaked by Mao's early policies. The four modernizations were the modernization of industry, agriculture, science and technology, and national defense. It was these "modernizations" that Deng would have to accomplish, focussing in particular on science and technology as a driver of the other three.

Today, as the result of Deng's courageous and bold path, China has emerged as the leading scientific nation on Earth, on the verge of major achievements in space exploration and exploitation (in the best sense of the term). Some of the greatest scientific and technological discoveries and innovations have come out of China in recent years, as Deng's science-driver principle has impelled China forward, as the United States, once the greatest scientific nation on Earth, continues on a path of self-destruction, under the treasonous mis-leadership of the past two presidencies of George W. Bush and Barack Obama.

taking root, many universities were reopened, and for the first time since 1965, students were allowed to take college entrance examinations. This first group of college entrants in over a decade, dubbed the "Class of 1977" (of which China's current Premier, Li Keqiang was one), became the basis for China's remarkable development since that time.

Already in 1975, Deng Xiaoping had begun to revive the China Academy of Sciences, bringing back many of the teaching cadres who had been sent to the countryside, many of whose members had died during the dark days of the Cultural Revolution.

The Chinese Government was prepared to temporarily accede to China becoming a low-wage producer as a prerequisite to its entry into the international system, but it also had a long-term strategy. It would agree to what were disadvantageous terms, but would forge the means by which it could work its way out of those conditions as quickly as possible, targeting key areas of science and technology in which it intended to "leapfrog to a higher stage of development."

Taking a page from the U.S. SDI program, China in 1986 developed its own "863 program for research and development." It chose seven key scientific areas in which it would put its resources, with the intent of making major scientific and technological breakthroughs in them. These areas were space, lasers, energy, biotechnology, new materials, automation, and information technology (IT). In 2009 the "863 program" was funding 110 new programs, including in IT, manufacturing, materials, resources and environment, earth observation satellites, transportation, biology, energy, and agriculture.

The Chinese Government also took another page from the U.S. model and established a National Science Foundation similar to the one in the United States. In 1997 China upgraded its science research program with a new program, the "973 Basic Research Program."

People's Republic of China

Deng came to power after the arrests of the Gang of Four, consisting of Mao's wife, Jiang Qing, and her associates, who campaigned against "bourgeois intellectuals." Deng immediately prioritized the development of a scientific and technological cadre over all other responsibilities and initiatives. Here, a poster denouncing the Four.

This program had the following objectives: (1) support multidisciplinary and fundamental research of relevance to national development; (2) promote frontline basic research; (3) support the cultivation of scientific talent capable of original research; and (4) Build high-quality interdisciplinary research centers.

Deng Xiaoping's 'Long March' of Science

Immediately upon being reinstated to all of his former party and government posts at the Third Plenum of the Tenth Party Congress on July 17, 1977, Deng made it clear that he intended to focus his priority attention on science, technology and education. He identified specific scientific programs—nuclear energy, computers, polymers, semi-conductors, astronautics, and lasers—as the first priorities.

At the time, China had 200,000 scientific and technological workers and the United States had 1.2 million. He sought every opportunity to meet with visiting Chinese-American scientists, including Lee Tsung-Dao, Yang Zhenning, and Samuel Ting—to discuss detailed plans. He insisted on placing top priority on building a nuclear accelerator to start training a generation of nuclear physicists and engineers. Although Deng had not attended university, his wife and three of his five children had all obtained degrees in physics from Beijing University.

Within a month of his return, Deng convened a Forum on Science and Education on Aug. 3, 1977 to begin the reorganization and expansion of all scientific institutions. He insisted that professional scientists be among the directors of all of the centers. He revived the Chinese Academy of Sciences (CAS) and founded a new Chinese Academy of Social Science (CASS). He reinstated the State Science and Technology Committee and ordered the drafting of a new Seven-Year Science Plan. During March 18-31, 1978, Deng held a conference on scientific and technological policy that inaugurated 108 new projects.

Deng Xiaoping insisted that Chinese scientists be provided with the necessary laboratory facilities, salaries, and resources to rapidly revive core work in the hard sciences. To accelerate the advancement of Chinese science, Deng sent many of the brightest Chinese students abroad to study in the best universities. He explicitly set out to reconstitute a meritocratic elite.

China's 'Iwakura Mission'

While Deng had, in his youth, spent time in France and in the Soviet Union, he had never been to the United States. He had no direct knowledge of the unique American System. He did, however, have a clear idea of that system, based on the mirror he saw in Meiji Japan, which

Deng had no direct knowledge of the American System, but he did study its application in Meiji Japan. Japan had learned the lessons of industrialization in the United States during the tour of the Iwakura Mission at the start of the Meiji period, 1871-1873. Here, the Iwakura Mission, led by Tomomi Iwakura (center), in London, 1870.

he did study. He used that knowledge to explore the global opportunities for China's rapid recovery from nearly two centuries of foreign oppression, first at the hands of the British and other European colonial powers, and then at the hands of militarist Japan.

Deng knew that there was another Japan that offered some valuable lessons to be learned. While Japan had learned the lessons of industrialization in the United States during the tour of the Iwakura Mission at the start of the Meiji period, 1871-1873, Deng was intent on learning from the Japanese experience as well as from the countries of the West in charting a path for China to follow in order to become a major industrial power.

In 1975, Deng Xiaoping made a five-day visit to France, where he received an opportunity to see first hand the tremendous advances that had been made by Western European states. Between 1977 and 1980, as he was relaunching China's economy, Deng sent many delegations abroad to study the methods of economic growth, scientific advance, and education. After hearing back from some of the first of the delegations, Deng noted that "Recently our comrades had a look abroad. The more we see, the more we realize how backward we are."

In the spring of 1978, Deng had dispatched four study tours to Eastern Europe, Hong Kong, Japan, and Western Europe (normalization with the United States would not be finalized until 1979). The most important of the study tours was led by Gu Mu, a respected economist, who brought a twenty-person ministerial delegation to Western Europe.

The delegates were stunned at the openness they encountered. They came back with initial offers for more than $20 billion in foreign investment in China. By June 30, 1978, Gu Mu had completed a written report to the Politburo. On July 6, 1978, the State Council convened a Forum on the Principles to Guide the Four Modernizations. It was led off by Gu Mu's report on the findings of his and other travel missions. The Forum ran through Sept. 9, allowing the findings to be disseminated widely throughout the government and party structures.

The foundations for China's spectacular growth were set by these initial actions by Deng Xiaoping, establishing the priority of scientific progress and advances in technology, and drawing upon the most advanced discoveries in the world.

China Shifts Gears

While the next decades would see the unfolding of Deng's vision, which he himself could observe before his death in 1997, the onset of the 2008 financial crisis created an entirely new situation which would again require wise and steady leadership.

With the onset of the 2008 financial blowout, it was clear that without a major reform of the entire system, a reform which the western financial elites were fighting tooth and nail, the tremendous export market for which China was producing would quickly disintegrate. There had to be a radical shift in order to prevent this crisis from leading to massive unemployment and social unrest in China itself. Fortunately, the onset of that period would find at the helm another leader, with the qualities of Deng Xiaoping, to steer China under the new conditions of world financial crisis, Xi Jinping.

Xi Jinping's father, Xi Zhongxun, had indeed been a protégé of Mao Zedong and a friend and protégé of Zhou Enlai. He held key posts in the Chinese Government, initially responsible for the western Shaanxi province and the area of Xi'an, one of the major regions along the Old Silk Road to Xinjiang province. This is where young Xi Jinping spent much of his childhood. In 1959 Xi Zhongxun was appointed Vice Premier, the youngest person ever to hold that position. But then, with the onset of the Cultural Revolution, he was purged in 1962. Xi Zhongxun spent the years of the Cultural Revolution working in a factory.

Young Jinping, unable to attend university, volunteered to serve in a small village in the north of China, performing all sorts of hard labor—carrying manure, hauling a coal cart, farming, and building dykes. Through his conscientious work and his dedication to the villagers, the young man won their trust and was elected village Party chief. Later he would serve in a variety of leading posts in Hebei, Fujian, Jiangsu, and Fujian provinces, and served as vice mayor of Shanghai before being transferred to Beijing for a more central posting.

With the demise of the Gang of Four in 1978, Xi Zhongxun was also called back to Beijing to help Deng Xiaoping reconstitute the social fabric of society after the devastation wrought by the Four. Even before the decision to initiate the "reform and opening up" as a nation-wide policy, Deng sent Xi Zhongxun to the city of Guangzhou (Canton) in the south of China, where he began the first experiment with economic liberalization. Largely due to the success of the Guangzhou experiment, Deng was able to initiate the reform on a national scale, leading to the rapid economic evolution of China as the world's foremost manufacturing center.

The record of Xi Zhongxun also clearly indicates

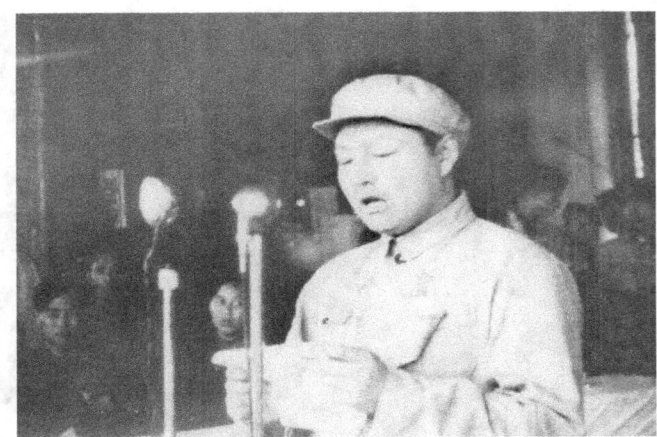

Xi Zhongxun, President Xi's father, was a protégé of Mao Zedong and a friend and protégé of Zhou Enlai. In 1959 he was appointed Vice Premier. With the onset of the Cultural Revolution, he was purged in 1962 and spent the years of the Cultural Revolution working in a factory. Here he addresses the crowd at a mobilization meeting in Xi'an in June 1949.

the tremendous affection in which he was held by the people he served as chief of Guangdong. Pictures of young Xi Jinping standing next to his father on many of his visits and meetings indicate that these were perhaps the important "study visits" that have helped inform Xi's views on China and its problems, its capabilities, and its future prospects. It was no doubt symbolic in many ways that Xi Jinping's first visit as Chinese president was to Guangzhou in Guangdong Province, location of the first experiment in the "opening up" and the region where his father had made his reputation as a reformer.

The Dream of Chinese Rejuvenation

The publication by the Chinese Government's Foreign Languages Press of a compilation of President Xi's speeches from November 2012 to June 2014, under the English title, *The Governance of China*, while not a biography, provides a great deal of insight into the mind of the man and into his intentions as the leader of the most populous nation in the world. In a speech given at a press conference at the 18th National Congress of the Central Committee of the Communist Party in November 2012, at which Xi Jinping formally took power, he gives an early introduction to his view of the path he felt China must take. "We are taking on this important responsibility for the nation," Xi said. He continued,

Ours is a great nation. Throughout 5,000 years of development, the Chinese nation has made

Xinhua/Lan Hongguang

Xi Jinping formally took power at the 18th National Congress of the Central Committee of the Communist Party in November 2012. Here, Xi participates in a panel discussion at the 18th National Congress.

significant contributions to the progress of human civilization. Since the advent of modern times our nation has gone through untold tribulations and faced its greatest perils. Countless people with lofty ideals rose up for the rejuvenation of the Chinese nation, but each time they failed. After it was founded in 1921, the Communist Party of China rallied and led the Chinese people in making great sacrifices, forging ahead against all odds, and transforming poor and backward China into an increasingly prosperous and strong nation, thus opening completely new horizons for national rejuvenation. Our responsibility is to rally and lead the entire Party and the people of all China's ethnic groups in taking on this task and continuing to pursue the goal of the rejuvenation of the Chinese nation, so that China can stand firmer and stronger among the world's nations, and make new and greater contributions to mankind.

One year later, the Central Committee also presented the program of continued reform which had, after careful study and under the direct leadership of Xi Jinping, been decided upon as the direction China would now take. The new situation, or "new normal" as it was called, required a change of emphasis in policy. While the opening up of the Chinese markets would continue

and there would be an increased reliance on "market mechanisms" to better allocate resources, there would also be a major revamping of the central government structure to make it more effective in giving direction to the Chinese economy.

"We should make good use of both the market, the 'invisible hand,' and the government, the 'visible hand,'" Xi told a study session of the Chinese Communist Party (CPC) Politbureau in May 2014, "to promote sustained and sound social and economic development." The "reform and opening-up" has always carried with it certain risks as the financial interests in the London-New York financial world would love to access the resources of China to continue to feed the monster of their financial bubble.

In his speeches, President Xi has continually warned of the dangers existing in the present crisis-ridden financial system. "Although we have a generally positive analysis of China's economic and social development," Xi told non-Party members at a symposium held by the CPC Central Committee in November 2013, "we must not underestimate the risk and challenges facing us now and in the near future. We must be aware that the pace of world economic growth will continue to be slow, the problem between sluggish demand and over-production capacity continues to grow, and domestic companies are troubled by rising costs and weaknesses in their capacity to innovate."

Creating a Knowledge-Based Society

At the same time, the situation required major changes in the functioning of the Chinese economy, which had to radically transform its mode of production in order to respond to the changing world situation. "Unbalanced, uncoordinated, and unsustainable development remains a big problem," Xi said. He added,

We are weak in scientific and technological innovation. The industrial structure is unbalanced and the growth mode remains inefficient. The development gap between urban and rural areas and between regions is still large, and so are income disparities. Social problems are markedly on the rise. Some people still lead hard lives. Formalism, bureaucratism, hedonism, and extravagance are serious problems. Some sectors are prone to corruption and other types of misconduct, and the fight against corruption remains a serious challenge for us. To solve these problems, the key lies in continuing the reform.

One of the key elements of the "new normal" is to increase productivity in the Chinese economy through technological advances. These advances can only come through technical innovations, the result of human creativity. Hence Xi's continual emphasis on innovation and creating a "knowledge-based economy." "Our scientists and engineers should bravely shoulder their responsibilities, overtake others, and find the right direction, to which they should stick," Xi told engineers and scientists in June 2014 at a General Assembly of members of the Chinese Academy of Sciences and the Chinese Academy of Engineering.

"They should have the courage and confidence to blaze new trails, overcome difficulties, and seek excellence, and audaciously make world-leading scientific and technological achievements." Xi looked at the problem, as he is prone to do, from the longer historical point of view. "I have been wondering about the reason why our science and technology gradually lagged behind from the late Ming (1368-1644) and early Qing (1644-1911) dynasties. Studies show that Qing Emperor Kangxi was very interested in Western science and technology," he said.

He then asked why this infusion of knowledge did not lead to a scientific renaissance in China. The problem, he said, was that, while the scholars learned a lot, "they did not apply what they had learned to social and economic development. Rather they simply talked about the knowledge." "To solve this problem," he said,

we must further scientific and technological system reform. Change mindsets and remove institutional barriers hindering scientific and technological innovation, properly handle the relationship between government and market, and better integrate science and technology with social and economic development. We must open a channel through which science and technology can boost industrial, economic, and national development. We must spur innovation with reform, accelerate the construction and im-

Emperor Kangxi (1654-1722) "was very interested in Western science and technology," according to Xi, who then asked why this infusion of knowledge did not lead to a scientific renaissance in China.

provement of a national innovation system, and let the well water of innovation gush out fully.

Some of the results of this initiative can clearly be seen in the tremendous advances China has made over a short span of time in its space exploration program, including its manned space exploration. It is also represented by the recent breakthroughs made in the development of nuclear fusion by China. President Xi has visited the Chinese nuclear fusion reactor at the Chinese University of Science and Technology in Hebei at least twice.

In connection with this, President Xi has also stressed the need for education, especially in the sciences. In a speech to a group of outstanding students on May 4, 2013, the anniversary of the May uprising in 1919, Xi said,

Young people must orient yourselves to modernization, the world, and the future, have a sense of urgency in updating your knowledge, study with great eagerness, lay a good foundation of basic knowledge while updating knowledge promptly, assiduously study theories while enthusiastically developing skills, and constantly enhance your competence and capabilities to meet the development needs of our times and the requirements of our undertaking. Innovation is the soul driving a nation's progress and an inexhaustible source of a country's prosperity. It is also an essential part of the Chinese national character. This is what Confucius meant when he said, "If you can in one day renovate yourself, do so from day to day. Yea, let there be daily renovation. Life never favors those who follow the beaten track and are satisfied with the status quo, and it never waits for the unambitious and those who sit idle and enjoy the fruits of others' work."

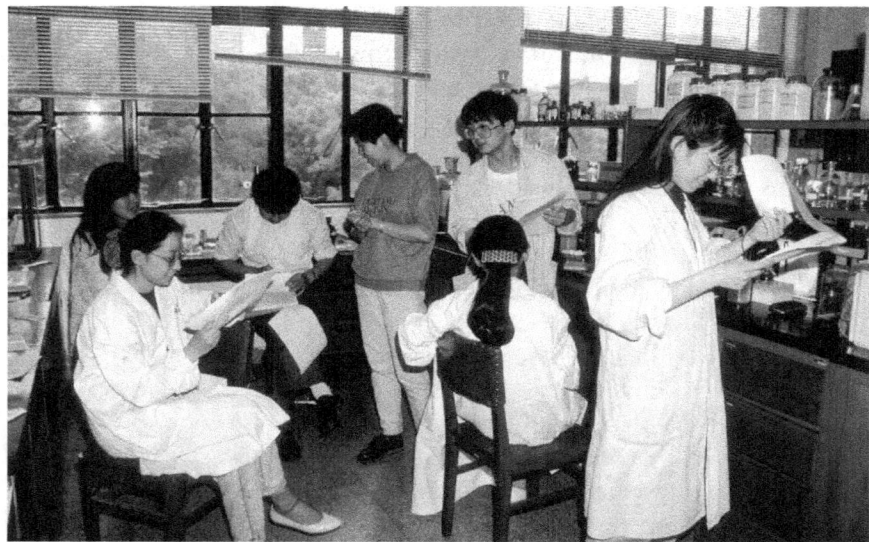

National Center for Biotechnology Information, U.S. National Library of Medicine

Xi told students in 2014, "Innovation is the soul driving a nation's progress and an inexhaustible source of a country's prosperity. It is also an essential part of the Chinese national character. This is what Confucius meant when he said, 'If you can in one day renovate yourself, do so from day to day.'" Students are at work here in the Max Planck Guest Laboratory, part of the Shanghai Institute of Cell Biology (CBI). The laboratory enables European scientists to work in China and stimulate contacts between Chinese and European scientists.

Lighting the Lamp of Wisdom

Xi often sprinkles his comments with sayings from Confucius, Mencius, and other ancient Chinese thinkers, which he has also incorporated into his own mental picture. He regards this tradition as representing the real greatness of China, which instils pride in the younger generation and provides the basis for that "dialogue of civilizations" which he has continually called for in his pursuit of helping his neighboring countries, both far and near, to achieve their own prosperity and greatness. Speaking to a study session of the CPC Politbureau, Xi said,

> During its 5,000-year history, the Chinese nation has created a brilliant and profound culture. We should disseminate the most fundamental Chinese culture in a popular way to attract more people to participate in it, matching modern culture and society. We should popularize our cultural spirit across countries as well as across time and space, with contemporary values and the eternal charm of Chinese culture.

And again in a speech at UNESCO headquarters on March 27, 2014:

> A single flower does not make spring, while one hundred flowers in full blossom bring spring to the garden. If there were only one kind of flower in the world, people would find it boring no matter how beautiful it was. Be it Chinese civilization or other civilizations in the world, they are all fruits of human progress.

The Nature of the Opposition

This general philosophical approach is no better symbolized than by the dramatic proposal for constructing the "One Belt, One Road" or the New Silk Road. China's emergence over the last few decades as a major world power, breaking the post-Cold War monopoly of the United States' position as the chief arbiter of international disputes, has unsettled many countries, particularly in the Asia-Pacific region. China is, of course, aware of the fact that it is the most powerful country in the region and that this has engendered some concerns among its less powerful neighbors, concerns that have been driven to fever pitch by the Obama Administration's reaction to China's rise by strengthening military commitments with its Cold

War allies and warning China that it remains a "player" in the region.

President Xi has been very clear that he understands the nature of these fears. Speaking to the Koerber Foundation in Berlin on March 28, 2014, Xi said:

> As China continues to grow, some people start to worry. Some take a dark view of China and assume that it will inevitably become a threat as it develops further. They even portray China as being the terrifying Mephisto who will someday suck the soul of the world. Such absurdity couldn't be more ridiculous, yet some people, regrettably, never tire of preaching it. This shows that prejudice is indeed hard to overcome. A review of human history shows that what keeps people apart are not mountains, rivers, or oceans, but lack of mutual understanding. As Gottfried Wilhelm Leibniz once observed, only the sharing of our talents will light the lamp of wisdom.

The New Silk Road Grows

The "One Belt, One Road" policy, which had been put on the table in its first manifestation 20 years ago by Lyndon LaRouche and Helga Zepp-LaRouche in collaboration with Chinese scholars—but had been kept in abeyance following the 1997 financial crisis—was resurrected by President Xi and made into the centerpiece of Chinese foreign policy. The policy aims at providing needed infrastructural investment to the surrounding countries and thereby transmitting some of the prosperity which China has achieved to the less well-off countries in the region and to the world.

While the initiative was originally focused on China's closest neighbors in Central Asia and in Southeast Asia, it has become—through the BRICS cooperation—a perspective that reaches far beyond the Asia-Pacific, to Africa, the Middle East, and Latin America.

During his own trip to the Middle East in February 2016, visiting Egypt, Saudi Arabia, and Iran, President Xi also introduced the Belt and Road as the means for transforming the economic situation in those countries, in the region now devastated by war. He underlined the importance of developing cooperation on energy, building infrastructure (particularly high-speed rail), and focusing on advanced technologies—nuclear energy,

WWW.NEWS.CN

Xinhua/Ju Peng

President Xi announced the New Silk Road initiative during a visit to Kazakhstan in September 2013. Xi and Kazakhstan's President, Nursultan Nazarbayev, are seen here in Astana, Kazakhstan's capital, during that visit.

space satellites and new energy. If the present tentative moves toward peace in Syria are to be effective, such a development program, a Marshall Plan for the Middle East, must be put into place. The Road and Belt Initiative could be the crux of such a plan.

But this New Silk Road, while emphasizing the connectivity of modern technology among the nations, also harks back to the spirit of the ancient Silk Road, where there was created an understanding between different nations and different cultures of their common interests. Speaking at Kazakhstan's Nazarbayev University in announcing the Silk Road Economic Belt in September 2013, President Xi underlined the broader cultural importance of this initiative:

> Throughout the millennia, the peoples of various countries along the ancient Silk Road have written a chapter of friendship that has been passed on to this very day. More than 2,000 years of exchanges demonstrate that on the basis of unity, mutual trust, equality, inclusiveness, mutual learning, and mutually beneficial cooperation, countries of different races, beliefs, and cultural backgrounds are fully capable of sharing peace and development. This is the valuable inspiration we have drawn from the ancient Silk Road.

The Promise and the Danger

Later in 2014, at the Fourth Summit of the Conference on Interaction and Confidence-Building Measures in Asia (CICA)—an organization proposed by Kazakh President Nursultan Nazarbayev with the goal of bringing the countries of Asia together in collaboration and consultation in the security realm—President Xi made a call to transform the organization into a forum for the overall security of Asia, moving away from the coalition-building in the region which had been the hallmark of the Cold War era, toward a policy of win-win cooperation. "Common security means respecting and ensuring the security of each and every country," Xi told the CICA members:

> Asia is a region of great diversity. The countries there differ in size, wealth, and strength. They vary in historical and cultural traditions as well as social systems, and have different security interests and aspirations. However, we are all part of the same Asian family. With our interests and security so closely intertwined, we will sink or swim together, and we are increasingly becoming a community of common destiny.

Security must be universal, Xi stressed. "We cannot have the security of just one or a few countries while leaving the rest insecure, in no way can we accept the so-called absolute security of one at the expense of the security of others."

President Xi's call will not be heeded as long as Obama is President and is intent on cementing a Cold War alliance policy aimed against China and Russia. The Belt and Road perspective entails a new paradigm of relations among nations, away from the geopolitics that is now rapidly leading to nuclear war.

While we don't see the quality of leadership in the West that has characterized China recently, we do hope that our future leaders will at least be smart enough to recognize that quality in others, and will be willing to work with the leaders of Russia, China, and India to overcome the present world crisis. Were that to occur, we could launch a new renaissance for mankind in which such leadership might be engendered as a matter of course in a population imbued with the spirit of achieving the common aims of mankind.

Oslo and the Present Moment in Syria

by *EIR* staff

Upon hearing the news in 1993 of the pending Oslo Accords, Lyndon LaRouche succinctly characterized the situation:

> The urgent thing here is that we must move with all speed to immediately get these economic development projects, such as the canal from Gaza to the Dead Sea, going immediately, because if we wait until we discuss this out, enemies of progress and enemies of the human race will be successful, through people like Ariel Sharon's buddies, in intervening to drown this agreement in blood and chaos.

Feb. 28—The past reaches out and speaks to us at this moment: The Oslo Accords for a settlement of the Palestinian-Israeli war failed because there was no economic development. The same will be true of Syria, if economic development isn't pushed through now.

Today, 23 years after Oslo, Palestine has no economy. The Palestinian Authority is bankrupt—on life support from donations that come from the European Union and erratically from the United States, along with occasional mega-donations from rich Arab states. Gaza and the West Bank are politically divided, and twice in the last eight years, Israel has bombed the hell out of Gaza, each time killing more than 1,500, the majority of them civilians. What little useful or productive capacity that was there, such as schools and food-processing factories, was destroyed or damaged and not rebuilt. Unemployment is as high as 70% among the young people in some parts of the Palestinian territories. There is no hope.

The advice that Lyndon LaRouche emphatically delivered right after the signing of the accords on Sept. 13, 1993, couldn't have been more clear: Start "moving the dirt" for construction by the end of September. The projects were brilliantly defined: LaRouche had worked over the previous decade with both Arab and Israeli leaders to define key projects.

The centerpiece for that development, which LaRouche called, "The Oasis Plan," was a set of multipurpose Dead Sea canals. They were not built then and still do not exist, but they are still key to the future of that area.

One canal was to run from the Mediterranean Sea to the Dead Sea, going through the Gaza Strip where, at the town of Gaza, a new port city could be constructed. The other, a "Red Sea/Dead Sea" canal, would run from the Dead Sea along the Wadi Araba, terminating at Aqaba on the Gulf of Aqaba on the Red Sea.

LaRouche insisted on giving nuclear power to the the Palestinians and Israelis for desalination, and several designs for safe, modular nuclear power plants had already been provided by companies including Germany's Siemens. Other companies, such as California's General Atomics, had provided designs for desalina-

Key (from map legend):
— Proposed Rail Lines
●─● Proposed Suez Canal Upgrade
═ Proposed Waterways for Power and Desalination
∷∷∷ Proposed Waterway Tunnel
❋ Proposed Nuclear Desalination Plants

LaRouche's "Oasis" Plan

One of the LaRouche Oasis Plan maps for Middle East development in the plan's 1995 version. LaRouche had included the plan in his 1975 publication, How the International Development Bank Will Work.

tion. The newly abundant water would be used for high-productivity agriculture, with Israel, the Palestinian territories, and Jordan cooperating.

These projects are described—with maps, illustrations, and additional comments from LaRouche—in the September 1993 *EIR* article by Marcia Merry titled, *Dust off the Blueprints for Mideast Development, Break Ground this Month*.

Now, Syria

Today, unless there is immediate economic development and reconstruction in the Middle East—conceived at the highest scientific and intellectual level—the ceasefire in Syria and the upcoming political talks are doomed, just as the Oslo Accords were. President Vladimir Putin knows that; President Bashar al-Assad knows that; President Xi Jinping knows that. All three of these presidents have spoken of the need for immediate reconstruction, and in his recent speech (January 2016) to the League of Arab Nations in Cairo, President Xi offered a perspective for renewed life for the Middle East.

Not only is reconstruction needed immediately, Xi said, to relieve the suffering of the hundreds of thousands of Southwest Asia's displaced refugees, huddled at the borders of the European Union, and of desperate civilians scraping for survival in war-devastated Syria, but it is the only path to really stopping terrorist recruitment.

"The key to overcoming difficulties is to accelerate development," Xi said. "Turmoil in the Middle East stems from the lack of development, and the ultimate solution will depend on development, which bears on everyone's well-being and dignity. It is a race against time and a struggle between hope and disillusion. Only when young people are able to live a fulfilled life with dignity through development, can hope prevail in their heart. Only then will they voluntarily reject violence, extremist ideologies, and terrorism."

China is offering a "win-win" strategy for all the countries of the region based on mutual interests, Xi said.

How Oslo Failed

On Sept. 13, 1993, after more than 45 years, the active war between the Palestinians and the Israelis fell quiet when Israeli Prime Minister Yitzhak Rabin and

Israeli Defense Forces

Where was the U.S. commitment to Middle East development when the first Oslo Accord was signed in September 1993? Here at the signing ceremony in Washington D.C. are Israeli Prime Minister Yitzhak Rabin (left), PLO Chairman Yasser Arafat (right), and U.S. President Bill Clinton.

Palestine Liberation Organization Chairman Yasser Arafat signed the "peace of the brave" Oslo Accord in hopes of stopping what threatened to become a "perpetual war" in the Middle East. The signing was done at the White House at the invitation of then-President Bill Clinton.

At dinner that night, Rabin made a profound historic statement, in the form of a toast to all who participated in the Oslo negotiations, asking that they tip their glasses to "those with the courage to change axioms." Peace was signed on paper, the Palestinian Authority was set up, but the axioms of the world financial oligarchy, of the British Empire whose evil Lord Balfour had turned historic Palestine into a cauldron of war with his "Balfour Declaration" of 1917, had not been changed.

The most hopeful part of the Oslo agreement was the inclusion of Annexes III and IV, which provided for Israeli-Palestinian Cooperation in Economic and Development Programs. These provisions reflected the longstanding input from LaRouche and others who argued that the creation of joint economic projects by Israel and Palestine working together to overcome the water shortage and general economic misery, was absolutely essential to building the good will between Palestinians and Israelis that would permit lasting peace.

But the economic development never happened. It

Creative Commons/International Committee of the Red Cross

The destruction in Syria, 2015. Without development, there can be no peace.

was not that the economic need was not recognized. It was sabotaged.

In fact, then-Israeli Foreign Minister Shimon Peres was explicit, advocating a "Marshall Plan" for the Mideast region. Speaking at the White House during the Oslo signing, Peres said:

> We shall support the agreement with an economic structure. We shall convert the bitter triangle of Jordanians, Palestinians, and the Israelis into a triangle of political triumph and economic prosperity.... Let us build a Middle East of hope, where today's food is produced, and tomorrow's prosperity is guaranteed, a region with a common market, a Near East with a long-range agenda.

Drowned in Blood

But, action did not follow, and as LaRouche had forecast, instead of peace and development, the region was drowned in blood.

The British empire agents of the right-wing Jewish settlers movement went for grabbing more and more land by expanding settlements in the areas defined by the Oslo agreement as future Palestinian land. Their real target was Rabin.

Terrorism was added to the slow death by lack of economic development.

In 1994, the first Israeli terrorist incident of mass murder was carried out by American-born West Bank settler, Baruch Goldstein, in Hebron. He was a member of the terrorist Kach movement. Goldstein entered a mosque and opened fire with an automatic rifle, killing some 30 Palestinians and wounding more than 100 others.

On Nov. 4, 1995, just after the Israeli Knesset approved the "land for peace" measures of Oslo, Prime Minister Rabin—the first Israeli-born Prime Minister—was assassinated by Yigal Amir, a radical Jewish settler who opposed peace with the Palestinians. Rabin, with Peres beside him, was leading a peace rally to celebrate the domestic passing of the Oslo agreement. The region has never recovered.

Michele Steinberg, Marcia Merry Baker, and Harley Schlanger contributed to this report.

Every Day Counts In Today's Showdown To Save Civilization

II. Destroy Wall Street

Not That Simple ...

Edited excerpts from Lyndon LaRouche's Dialogue with the Manhattan Project of Feb. 27.

Question: Hi, Lyn, K— from the Bronx. Very good. I'm having a terrible time wrapping my brain around what's going on in Syria and I'm here today to have you help me out with it.

There appears to be two factions in the government, one for peace and one for war. What draws my attention to that possibility is Kerry's cooperation with Putin and China in creating a working relationship with the United States, Putin, and China. I have been prejudiced against Kerry and now see him working for a ceasefire in Syria as very confusing to me. What is Kerry's position with Obama? As Secretary of State he's expected to represent the President. What is Obama's position with this cooperation of Kerry with Putin? I'm under the impression that the agreement Kerry signed was created by Putin. It's hard for me to not to wonder if there aren't threats going to Kerry. Does this weaken Obama to the degree that will give someone or some group the courage to remove him? How do you see the British dealing with this?

LaRouche: Well, that's quite a package of complications. The complications however are not in and of themselves a problem. It's only when you try to mix them up. That's when the problem comes up. Because the matter is that there are different parties, there're different factors under consideration. For example ... Just to give you an example. What has happened recently is that there is a collapse of the trans-Atlantic commu-

nity. The trans-Atlantic community is in a disaster mode.

On the other hand you have the Russian mode and the Chinese mode and other things related to the same which are on the upscale. So, obviously, there's not a complementarity of voices, but rather a conflict, a very significant conflict. Do you want to live or die? That's the difference. If you want to follow Obama, if you want to work with the British royal family, then you're doomed. If you want to get a succession for a new world system and you're able to do it, together with Russia, China, India and so forth,— this is a different voice. The one voice, the old voice, is the evil voice. It's the evil voice of stupidity and corruption. That's the voice of Obama and the British.

On the other hand what Putin represents and what China represents, right now,— and now India coming in,— in a very significant way, in a resurrection kind of way, and these things are going to develop.

So there is no monotone in this process. The question is the crisis. Are you going to die? Are you going to

Putin, China, India, represent the way for a new world system. Russia has unveiled plans, a part of which is depicted above, to build a city for 5,000 year-round residents 1,000 miles from the North Pole.

live? And that's it, two voices. One voice, are you going to die? Second voice, are you going to live? And when you look at things in that way, as I do, it becomes relatively clear. I don't want to have anything to do with Wall Street. I don't want to have anything to do with that bunch. I don't want to have anything to do with Obama. On the other hand, there're certain people of the world who, I say, are valuable. We say that the trans-Atlantic community is terrible. It's a sinkhole, all kinds of evil. While on the other hand, what you get with Putin and get with China and get with India, you are now almost on the road towards Paradise. And that's the difference.

They Are Doomed

Question: Good afternoon, Lyn. A— here in New York. I missed you Thursday. I had a bad connection. I think we're a little better today, I hope.

The people of the United States are doomed, doing things in their behavior to destroy the meaning of their lives. Here, one of many tailgate parties before a football game.

I wanted to talk with you about,— you've stated that our mission, our purpose is to engage people, bring people into the process of development into a unified purpose. Of course, that means you're going to end imperialism—a very historic, monumental move—and allow mankind to continue in the path that's being expressed by the nations we talk about all the time, and the United States can join that and a happy future can be realized for mankind, well beyond our lifetimes.

And that we also state, I love the line, that you say "we don't need a great many people. We need a few great people," and I go, "yes but they're hard to find"! and then, I've been thinking about that, and the frustrations that seem to come from that. And I go now to a circle that I'm familiar with and see fairly regularly, and I would often find myself complaining: Well, you know, they just don't get it. I'm talking to them and I'm saying things. And one person in particular is a black man from Northwest America, and I've known him for some years. and it wasn't until just yesterday, that he expressed to me that—you know I always thought he was a jock and had a jock mentality—and he revealed to me,— he said, "you know, I was an honor student with a scholarship to go into engineering school. And as I was preparing for that, my family collapsed, father drinking, broken home and so on." And he says "it was at that time that I just decided to turn jock."

I'm raising this because he had this camouflage about him; there's this disparity in the population, where we've made assumptions or think we're looking at something in a person that we really aren't. Now this was important and very useful of course, because now I think I know what he wants to hear, because I know actually who he is and what he abandoned, years ago. But there were indications of this before in the times that we would exchange.

So, in achieving that mission I just want to share that type of thing that I think is very common, and will allow me now to be more effective in finding that the people can realize that they're great within themselves if I let them.

LaRouche: Well, that's not that simple. The question is, are you going to be a contribution in your actions, is this going to be a contribution to the future of man? Now, how do we locate this thing?

The people of the United States are doomed. Right now, as of now, they are doomed. They're doing all the things that are necessary in their behavior, to destroy themselves and to destroy the meaning of their lives. What we're seeing now, as you see now in the experiences which are clinically shown in this matter,— everybody in general as a category, not as every individual, but as a category; the category of the people of the United States *and* of also other areas of that area, are doomed by what they believe in and what they work for. Now, they deceive themselves on this issue.

What you have now, what you have in Russia and India, as opposed to the trans-Atlantic community: The trans-Atlantic culture is now in a falling mode of self-destruction. On the other hand, Russia, China, India, and certain other countries, represent a commitment to an improvement in the condition of man's life.

So it's not a question of who you are and how you change your tricks. That's a religious fakery, which is a very popular one. To say "Oh I'm corrected now, I'm corrected now." The question is, what are you creating, in terms of the future of mankind? And that's the issue. That you can perfect yourselves or improve yourself in some way, and thus find your solution for all your sufferings and so forth,— that doesn't work.

rustwire.com

Skilled working people in the United States are now rotting away, in a self-inflicted dying process. Formerly productive people are now becoming degenerate. Above, the abandoned Carrie blast furnace in Pittsburgh, Pa.

The difference is that there is a force which is upside the individual type. And that force is the question of true creativity, mankind's true creativity. And what we're having is,— the United States and the trans-Atlantic system is now *Satanic. It's in a Satanic collapse mode.* On the other hand, Russia, China, and India and so forth, actually fit in generally into an upturn mode. The United States and all of the trans-Atlantic community is ready to go into a deep and prolonged collapse, something like the collapse of the Roman Empire. Whereas another part of the civilization during the same period was in a rising mode; which is not an improvement mode, it was the directly opposite mode.

And if we're going to solve the problems which face the United States and other nations right now, that is the kind of distinction we have to make.

Just look at one thing, for example, as a clinical case. We have people who used to be working people. They had certain practical skills, more or less good practical skills. Recently, under Obama's influence, what has happened, is the people who used to be the working people, the skilled working people, are now rotting away. They're dying. They're in a self-inflicted dying process. The only thing we can do about them is

to try to get them out of it. *But!* if you look at the policy of the people of the United States, this so-called class of persons, they're not going to make it, unless some miracle comes in and saves them. They are dying! They're committing suicide, mass suicide on drugs and all kinds of behavior; a group of people who used to be productive in earlier forms of life are now becoming characteristically degenerate, self-degenerating.

So the problem is now, then what do you have to say? Well, what can you do? Do you want to try to improve people's behavior? That won't work. Because behavior is a subterfuge. It's not a perfect thing. But what happens, you find, that in practice what Putin is doing, what China is doing, what India is now doing, and others, is actually the *road to success*. Whereas the existence of the trans-Atlantic society is a plunge into destruction, like the fall of the Roman Empire. And these are the considerations which have to be examined.

Something That Has a Meaning

Question: Good afternoon, Mr. LaRouche, I'm T— from Manhattan, recently retired and enjoying very much singing in the bass section of our chorus, *Messiah*. Reminds me of the time that Paderewski represented Poland at the Versailles Conference, and went to pay a visit to the French Prime Minister Clemenceau, and Clemenceau asked, "By the way, are you any relation to the pianist?" and Paderewski said, "I am the pianist." [Laughter.] And Clemenceau said, "My Lord, what a falling off was here? From greatest pianist in the world to merely the head of a nation."

Well, the reason I'm rejoicing about the chorus is that the choral counterpoint is a demonstration to me of how democracy works. Every voice is precious. Every voice gets to lead, every voice gets to support. And there are obvious social implications to this. And my question to you is, that I know that from the beginning you have purposed that the chorus dynamic shall be expanded to a wider social and political sphere. I'm not quite sure about the mechanisms that would accomplish this expansion of energy. Could you say a few words about that, please?

LaRouche: She just presented it in terms of her presentation of the concluding parts of her report today. [Referring to the choral work before the town-hall meeting.] There is something which has a meaning; it's not something which improves from in itself. It's something which improves from outside itself. And it's when people change their outlook on life that they are able to see a future, whereas in other circumstances people can't understand what life means. And that's the difference. So there has to be an internal creative motive, which seizes the soul, so to speak, of the individual, and then the individual would not want to do anything that befouls the goal of the action.

In other words, the question is, people will go out and try to be showmen; they try to be successful by inspiring people and uplifting them in some way or other. But on other hand, the real thing, is what does the individual,— in the process of directing the course of self-development,— what do they do in terms of the future of mankind? That's what's important. And therefore, the people who do good things,— and you have some people who do good things in part, but don't do very well overall in terms of achievement. And it's the overall improvement which is crucial. Many people have adaptations to these things, but they don't have what we might call qualified, deep commitment to these beliefs. That's what the difference is.

China TV

Russia, India, and China have a mission orientation leading to the commitment to a development process. This is exemplified by China's development of its space program. Here, Chinese astronaut Wang Yaping, on June 19, 2013, is giving a lecture from space broadcast on Chinese TV.

Subtle Things, Not Simple Things

Question: Hello Lyndon. I've been an avid follower of your work for years, and today I come with a complete proposal and wanted to share it with you. United National Anti-War Coalition and a number of other organizations have endorsed a protest in front of the United Nations in New York on Sunday, March 13. And the focus of the protest is going be both domestic and foreign policy issues that are so close to the ideas that the LaRouche PAC has been promoting for decades. It's a protest against measures that would bring on World War III. It's a protest against policies of confrontation with China and Russia; it's a protest against bank deregulation and other financial measures that brought on the global financial crisis.

And so we're trying to bring together different parts, from the left, the right, the entire political spectrum that's opposed to the Democratic and Republican mainstream, that has brought this country to the crisis point at which it is right now. So, the question is what do you think about that idea, the idea of holding that protest?

LaRouche: Okay, let me give you a little anecdote on this thing. I'm acquainted,— I never personally spoke to him,— but I have been active with him in part of his career,— Putin. Now, Putin is a survivor from a set of families which were largely brutalized by the Nazis, when the Nazi fight was going on. And most of these people died, they were murdered, just by the process of the conditions. And what happened was, then you had Putin who developed himself with a mission orientation; and the mission orientation is centered in his awareness of his immediate family's mass death in the household because of the Nazi fight. And he fought that course.

He has a dimension, which is what? The dimension is, for him,— India is important, China is much more important because of the awareness of this thing. The role of China in developing the space program, which was a development within my lifetime period of development. Now we have in this whole Eurasian area, from Russia, across Asia, and we have a development process now, which is a rich development, which is not limited to the experience of the people who are participating in that development. But that rather they are dedicated to the *future* of mankind, beyond their own lives, and the ability of their own lives. And the consistency is that Putin's life,— because here he's one of the survivors of that group in Russia in that period, when the Nazis were hitting so hard against that area,— and he came back at that, against the forces of evil, not just evil against him, but evil against mankind generally. And

therefore the future of mankind is something which lies in what mankind can make as a creative contribution to the future of mankind; that is, to be devoted to the realization of something that mankind will not *ever* fully, accurately achieve in its own life.

And the whole purpose of mankind is the ability of mankind to make discoveries, which the discoverer will never fully harvest, but only the persons who are of that spirit of behavior will be able to deliver an example of what is necessary, for the future of mankind.

These are much more subtle things; they are not simple things. Just take this whole thing of Russia, just as an example. In this Russian case, the mass murder that occurred in Russia,— and it was mostly battlefield issues, if you know the history of the warfare in the Second World War in Russia, and you see that people gave massively, the very existence of their lives, and worked and were dedicated to the purpose of producing for the *next* generation which would be able to accomplish the missions which the present generations had failed to accomplish. It's that passion which goes beyond explanations of technicalities and so forth. These are things I think are the most important things.

Japanese Economist Kotegawa: Shut Down the Investment Banks

by Mike Billington

Feb. 29 (EIRNS)—The former Japanese Ministry of Finance official who had major responsibility for dealing with Japan's 1997-98 financial breakdown, told *EIR* this week that the current global crisis can not be resolved by the methods used to resolve that Japanese crisis, and certainly not by the Obama measures which totally failed to resolve the destruction caused by the 2008 crash in the United States.

Rather, he said, the entire investment bank structure must be shut down, across the trans-Atlantic region, both to stop their financial warfare operations on behalf of the London and New York financial oligarchy, but also because they are in fact clinically bankrupt.

Daisuke Kotegawa was an official at the Ministry of Finance in Japan when the Japanese banking system exploded in November 1997, after two banks and two securities firms went under (the seventh largest and the fourth largest, just as Bear Stearns and Lehman Brothers were the seventh and fourth largest in the United States). He was one of the primary officials responsible for dealing with that crisis.

In a Feb. 28 interview with *EIR,* he contrasted the tough measures taken by Japan to deal with their crisis, to the lack of any serious measures in the United States after 2008, which, he argues, is the reason that the crisis has returned in the western banking system with a vengeance, threatening the catastrophic collapse of the entire western financial system.

"Since Japan introduced the modern banking system about 150 years ago, after the Meiji Restoration," Mr. Kotegawa said, "it has been our principle to establish the depositors' confidence in our finance system. Those engaged in the banking system had to try their best to establish trust among all their depositors.

"So, when I had to deal with the liquidation of one

EIRNS/Christopher Lewis

Daisuke Kotegawa was one of the primary Japanese officials responsible for dealing with the crisis at the time of the November 1997 explosion of the Japan banking system. Unlike during the 2008 U.S. crisis, Japan took tough measures.

of the major Japanese securities houses, Yamaichi Securities, the main principle was to try to maintain the reputation of our financial system, as well as the reputation of the supervisory authority. We tried to avoid Japan's becoming the epicenter of a world economic crisis.

"Using the long three-day weekend of Nov. 22-24, we unwound all the trans-border transactions that Yamaichi had, including a substantial amount of derivatives that they had through their branch in London. So accordingly, although the government had to take the burden of a huge amount of money to rescue these institutions, the crisis in Japan did not affect other countries whatsoever."

The key to preserving confidence, he said, was to impose "a very rigid examination system of the balance sheets of the banks. Because left alone, bankers would never tell you the real story. So we conducted a very rigid examination, and made public how much public money would be needed to clean up the balance sheets of our banks. And we actually put in taxpayers' money, enough to clean up their non-performing loans. This sent a message to our depositors that our banks were now healthy. This is very important.

"In the case of the United States," Mr. Kotegawa added, "you never conducted this kind of investigation. So there was no assurance at all among the people involved in various businesses that the banking system was healthy. Instead, you started so-called stress tests, which is completely wrong, because if the status of bank assets at the outset of the stress tests is not properly reported, then everything is assumption."

Most important, he said, is the fact that Japan threw many leading bankers in jail. "We put in the taxpayers' money to rescue these banks. but at the same time we actually pursued the responsibility and the liability and the crimes of those bankers who pushed the Japanese government to use that large portion of taxpayers' money. So we actually investigated their financial reports back five or six years, and found a large amount of window-dressing by those banks, and put members of the boards of the failed banks in jail. This has not been done at any of the United States' banks, nor, I think, in any European country. Without this kind of investigation, there is no sense of fairness among taxpayers nor among depositors."

EIR asked Mr. Kotegawa about the demands from Wall Street during that Japan crisis.

"First of all," he responded, "at that time we were under very heavy pressure from our friends in the United States to clean up the balance sheets of our banks as fast as possible, people such as Tim Geithner and Larry Summers. They sent us a message that the Japanese banking system should take a hard landing. This means three things: 1) No bail-out of the banks; 2) maintain short selling; and 3) use mark-to-market on the bank assets [i.e., value the assets at their real value on the market, not at their inflated face value]. But unfortunately, when the Lehman shock started [the 2008 so-called sub-prime crisis in the United States], all of these three principles were breached by Larry Summers and Timothy Geithner themselves."

Asked if Japan followed the advice of Summers and Geithner, Mr. Kotegawa said: "After the huge shock at the end of 1997 and 1998, we followed this advice from the United States, but we found that this was not the right policy. We actually kept this principle for the first two years, and then changed the policy in 2000. One thing I'd like to emphasize, is why it is so important to punish those bank officers, based upon my own experience in investigating various cases back in Tokyo: Those bankers would not admit that they made mistakes. And if they do not admit they made mistakes, then they will repeat the same mistakes again and again. And that is now actually happening in the whole financial system in the United States and in Europe. They are still engaged in the same kind of very risky transactions, such as huge amounts of derivatives."

Finally in 2000, Japan dropped the policies demanded by Wall Street. It put strict limits on short selling, and bailed out some of the viable banks which were not weighted down with derivatives. It retained the mark-to-market accounting. "When the Lehman shock started," Mr. Kotegawa said, "it was your Congress which actually told the association of accounting firms to relax mark-to-market accounting for a while."

The Current Crisis

Mr. Kotegawa told *EIR* emphatically that the current general breakdown of the entire western financial system could not be dealt with by the methods used in Japan. Simply shutting down bankrupt banks and jailing the criminals running them, while necessary, is not enough when the entire western banking system has been turned into a gambling casino, as the result of the takedown of Glass-Steagall.

What is required, he said, is "large scale, world-scale fiscal stimulus, such as the one introduced by China in the form of the AIIB. If this is done, this would create real demand and create new employment."

He emphasized that the entire investment bank structure must be eliminated: "We should destroy all of these—close down all of these investment banks. If you conduct a real examination of the balance sheets of these banks, using the method of 'line sheets' examination, this would surely reveal that these investment banks are actually insolvent."

This would be accomplished by the restoration of Glass-Steagall, as a first step to shutting down Wall Street. Nothing less can prevent the implosion of the now two quadrillion dollar derivatives bubble dominating Wall Street and the City of London, and the death and destruction that is already sweeping Europe and the United States under the tyrannical rule of Wall Street under Obama.

III. Extra-Terrestrial Imperative

There Are *No* Limits to Growth— Mankind Must Conquer Space!

by Kesha Rogers

Address to the Schiller Institute Town Hall meeting, Feb. 27, 2016, that featured Kesha Rogers, Tom Wysmuller, and Megan Beets. Video of the entire meeting is here.

Hello everyone. Thank you for joining us for today's proceedings. I would like to welcome everyone to this policy forum, which is being hosted by the Schiller Institute. I would like to thank our international audience for watching as our proceedings are streamed online. The title of our discussion is, "There Are *No* Limits to Growth: Mankind Must Conquer Space."

Before we begin, we have a special musical offering, our National Anthem. [Choral presentation follows, of verses 1, 2, and 4 of the *Star-Spangled Banner.*]

I will be joined on this panel by Tom Wysmuller, a member of The Right Climate Stuff, and a member of the NASA Alumni League. I would like to give a special thanks to Tom for joining us—he came a very long way, drove here, and the guy's phenomenal [laughter, applause]—and for all that he and his group, The Right Climate Stuff, are doing to educate the population around what's going on. I'm also joined on the panel today by Megan Beets, a leader of

Kesha Rogers: *"Whats happened to our ability to reason? We have allowed limitations to be placed on it."*

the LaRouche Policy Institute, the LaRouche Science & Research Team.

I want to make a few remarks on why we are here and what we seek for you to take from this discussion. First of all, I have been a national leader in the fight to revive the true intentions of our space program, since the egregious cuts and attacks by our current administration on our manned space program and the cancelling of the Constellation program back in 2010.

To understand what is truly at stake, one need not look at simply what the budget cuts were or why some programs were chosen over others. The real attack is what German space flight pioneer Krafft Ehricke would have called it, the attack on "man's extraterrestrial imperative."

Now, Krafft Ehricke was a brilliant man, a genius, and he can be looked up to as an inspiration in understanding why we fight, and must fight, for a space program that identifies the true intention of mankind, and what must become of the future of mankind in conquering space. Ehricke understood, first of all, that placing limitations on the imaginative and creative progress of mankind was the biggest attack against achieving the goals of conquering space. He actually put forth a schematic that he addressed from the standpoint that if people did not fulfill man's true extraterrestrial imperative and allowed limitations to be put on human progress, then you would see a society that would be attacked by war, starvation, and famine, and would have negative growth.

That is the policy which we're fighting against right now, with the limits to growth that have been placed on mankind, this idea that there are limited resources, that there are too many people in the world. And that's what you are really fighting against right now: This Malthusian idea of limited resources, this population reduction policy, including the environmentalist fraud that there is man-made global warming. And one of the key attacks of this whole way of thinking is on the creative progress of mankind.

To combat this fraud, one cannot just refute made-up "hockey stick models" and deal with ice core samples. It is necessary to get at the root of the matter: What is the realization of man's true self? That is what the fight is, right now. There are many people out there who can present the scientific basis as to why the man-made global warming claims are a hoax. But the question—and what we seek to bring out in this entire discussion—is what is the attack on the creative nature of mankind? Why is the extraterrestrial imperative of mankind being attacked?

Now, to understand that, consider one of the ideas put forward in a conference held in 1985—31 years ago—by the Schiller Institute, the organization that is sponsoring this event, and that was founded by Helga Zepp-LaRouche. This was the memorial conference honoring the life of Krafft Ehricke. The title of that conference was, "The Age of Reason in a World of Mutually As-

Tom Wysmuller

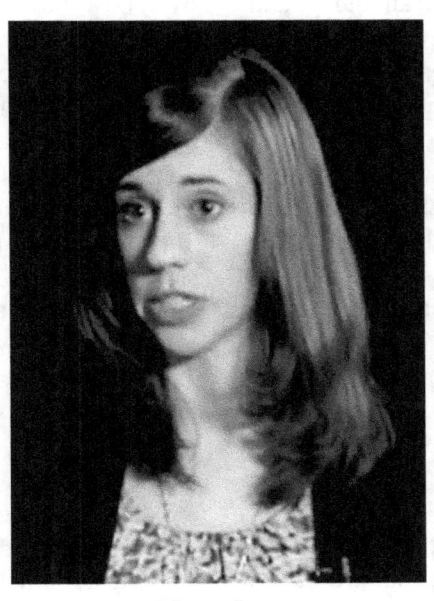

Megan Beets

sured Survival and Space Colonization."

I think that conference characterized where we are today: The point that we face today, is that we have lost the ability in our society to reason. When we take away our space program, the manned space program, and particularly the implications of what it truly represents, then what happens to the creative imagination of your society? What happens to the ability of your society, of mankind, to reason as beings who are seeking to further develop the intention of our Creator, the intention of the creative process of the universe? And to discover more, where mankind must go, the future that mankind must create. And at that conference, Mrs. LaRouche characterized Krafft Ehricke as one who understood that lifting the eyes of the world to the stars, and the industrialization and colonization of the Moon and Mars, were expressions of the intention of mankind and mankind's extraterrestrial imperative.

I'd like to read a quote from Krafft Ehricke that characterizes this fight against the limitations put on mankind. Ehricke says, "The world of modern industrial man is no more closed within the biosphere than it is flat. Preservation cannot be limited to the environment at the expense of human growth. Human growth must aim at nothing less than the achievement of a human living standard for all, the preservation of both environment and civilization hinges on technology, and its translation into industry. Many technologies are needed to overcome the present apparent limits to growth, but the one underlying, unambiguous technology that makes many other industrial technologies possible, either directly or by spinoffs, is space technology." Very important.

Now, the age of reason, the idea of what is the true nature of man,—

How did we come to understand and realize man's own true self, but through the development of space? And this is what Krafft Ehricke clearly understood and why we fight today. As Ehricke said, "there is no one and nothing under the natural laws of the universe that can place limitations on man, except man himself." Now that's important, because the problem is, what's happened to our ability to reason? We have allowed limitations to be placed on it.

So that's what we have to get at right now; that's what we have to get at in the discussion, and it is what we are addressing now with the national and international campaign that I have launched to revive our space program. We are launching what I would call the "awakening of a sleeping giant."

EIRNS/Stuart Lewis

In January 1985, five months before the Krafft Ehricke Memorial Conference, the Schiller Institute organized a rally of ten thousand in Washington for a science-driver space program of U.S.-Soviet cooperation for mutually assured survival, the Strategic Defense Initiative.

It's very interesting—I'll just make one report here—that there was a hearing in Congress a few days ago, with the former director of NASA Mike Griffin and also former astronaut Gene Cernan, and others. You can tell from the testimony that there is an understanding of this creative identity and a hunger for its expression, for mankind to once again act on its extraterrestrial imperative—to conquer space, recognizing that that is the only thing that is truly going to bring nations together.

We will have some further discussion of what other nations are doing to carry out this true imperative of mankind.

When you have these speakers addressing the Congress and saying that President John F. Kennedy, if he saw our space program today, would be rolling over in his grave, you have to think about that: They are *absolutely* correct! And the problem is, we also have an administration that is spitting on the grave of President Kennedy when it puts forth such a policy.

We have to come together as a national and international community to recognize again, that we have a mission for mankind. Other nations are starting to rec-

ognize this, and the United States has to be brought into that mission for mankind.

I want to end with a statement by economist and statesman Lyndon LaRouche, who also spoke at the 1985 conference, because I think it characterizes very well how we once again gain the age of reason. He said that Krafft Ehricke understood that the mission of mankind in colonizing and exploring space, lies in removing all limitations. In his presentation to the conference, he characterized the age of reason as the "intent of the Creator that mankind's destiny is to become mankind in the universe." He said, "There, in the stars, lies mankind's entry into the long-awaited Age of Reason, when our species sheds at last the cultural residue of the beast."

And that's what we have to shed, because people have become bestial; you have a culture that has been destroyed. Just look at the conditions of life on the planet right now. We have to awaken in the spirit of the population a new paradigm, a new direction for mankind. And you see that we're on the verge of doing that, if you look at what's going on in some other countries and the fight that's even taking place here in the United States.